FREEZER
COOKBOOK

Consulting Editor:
Valerie Ferguson

southwater

Contents

Introduction

The freezer is an invaluable piece of kitchen equipment. Convenience foods are useful, but it is worth making space for some specially cooked freezer dishes. Far from increasing time spent in the kitchen, this practice will reduce it. For example, prepare a double quantity of a casserole – one for now and one for later. Then, when you don't feel like cooking or you are short of time, a home-cooked meal is to hand. As many dishes can be defrosted quickly in the microwave, you may not even have to think ahead. Indeed, some things are better cooked from frozen.

A vast range of cooked dishes and fresh produce can be frozen, though there are a few things that simply don't work. It is vital to pack food properly, and information about how to do this follows. Freezing is the best way of preserving food and is ideal for prepared dishes, as the flavour is retained and, in some cases, it actually improves during storage.

This book is packed with perfect freezer recipes, with at-a-glance guides to defrosting and reheating. Whether you are planning a party, require a supply of family suppers or simply want to take time off from the kitchen, turn to your freezer.

Practical Advice

The Freezer

There are several different kinds – chest, upright and fridge freezers – and a huge range of sizes. Choose one that suits your family's needs, as a freezer works more economically and efficiently when well stocked.

The temperature inside the freezer should be below -18°C/-0.4°F. To test, put a freezer thermometer in a drawer or basket and leave overnight. If the temperature is not correct, adjust the thermostat – the higher the number, the colder the freezer will be.

Avoid opening the door or lid frequently, especially when freezing fresh foods. Never leave the door ajar. Always make sure that cooked dishes are cold before putting them in the freezer, and use the fast-freeze switch.

Using the freezer drawers or baskets ensures a proper circulation of air. However, if necessary, they can be removed and foods stacked directly on the shelves. Do not fill the freezer over the load line.

Defrosting

The golden rule is freeze fast and defrost slowly. Rapid freezing ensures that the ice crystals forming in the food, which is what preserves it and slows down the action of enzymes and bacteria, are small. Slow defrosting in a cool place or in the fridge helps to preserve the texture.

Defrosting in the microwave is suitable for some but not all dishes. Guidelines are given with all recipes. Follow the manufacturer's instructions for defrosting and reheating, as microwaves vary considerably.

Once defrosted, the food can deteriorate very rapidly, so it should be cooked as soon as possible. Never freeze food that has already been frozen and defrosted. Check that fresh foods have not been commercially frozen first if you are planning to freeze them. Dishes that have been prepared and cooked from defrosted frozen ingredients, however, can be safely frozen.

Flavourings

Most flavours become more pungent with freezing, so it is important to be light-handed with seasoning, particularly strong and powerful-tasting ones such as garlic and chillies.

Left: Plastic containers, clear film, kitchen foil, thermometer and freezer bags.

Packing Food for Freezing

It is important that food is protected from freezer burn, which shows as unattractive and discoloured patches on the surface. While the food is still safe to eat, the texture and appearance will have deteriorated.

Above: Plastic dishes from ready-made foods can be re-used time and time again.

Rigid containers are ideal for stews, casseroles and soups, and are also useful for individual tarts and cakes. Foil trays with cardboard lids and freezer-to-microwave dishes are widely available.

Otherwise, use freezerproof plastic dishes. Stews, pies and casseroles can also be frozen in the dishes in which they were cooked, covered with foil or two layers of clear film, provided that the dishes are freezerproof.

If you are going to defrost and finish cooking in the microwave, always use microwave-safe containers. If you cannot spare the dish for the time it will be in the freezer, an alternative may be to line the dish with foil or two layers of clear film, freeze it, then turn it out and wrap it securely. Return the food to the original dish – without the foil or clear film – for defrosting and reheating or cooking. Tarts and flans can be frozen covered with foil or two layers of clear film and then transferred to plastic freezer bags when frozen. Plastic freezer bags are also useful for freezing fresh fruit and vegetables.

Always label containers before freezing – do not rely on your memory. It is useful to add the date of freezing. Use freezerproof labels and pens.

Unsuitable Foods

Some foods cannot be frozen. These include the following:

- Whole eggs, but beaten eggs, either together or separated, can be frozen.
- Dishes made with gelatine can be frozen, but tend to liquefy if kept for longer than two weeks.
- Fruit and vegetables with a high water content, such as cucumber and bananas, cannot be frozen successfully. Strawberries freeze well if they are to be incorporated into a dish, such as a mousse, but their texture will not be suitable for using whole.
- Homogenized skimmed and semi-skimmed milk may be frozen, but full-fat milk separates. Cream with a high fat content can be frozen, but not single cream or soured cream. When using as a garnish to a dish, such as goulash, it is best to add cream after defrosting and reheating.
- Sauces, such as mayonnaise.

Freezing Tips

Freezing Mushrooms

To preserve mushrooms quickly and effectively, consider freezing them. Firmer varieties are best, such as shiitake, blewits, horn of plenty, chanterelle, closed field and horse mushrooms. To thaw, immerse briefly in boiling water before using.

1 Bring a saucepan of salted water to the boil and line a tray with greaseproof paper. Ensure mushrooms are free from grit and infestation, then trim and slice thickly if large. Simmer the mushrooms in the boiling water for 1 minute.

2 Drain well and open freeze for 30–40 minutes on the tray. Turn into plastic freezer bags, label and return to the freezer for up to 6 months.

Freezing Berries

Most berries freeze well, especially if they are to be used for mousses and fools. Open freeze perfect specimens in a single layer on a baking sheet, then pack into rigid containers. Damaged berries can be puréed and sieved, then sweetened with sugar or honey.

Freezing Herbs

Culinary herbs, finely chopped and packed in measured amounts with water in ice-cube trays, lose little of their flavour when frozen, and are ready for almost immediate use. This is a particularly good storage method for herbs, such as coriander, that do not dry successfully.

Basic Recipes

Tomato Sauce

Quickly defrosted and packed with flavour, this sauce is a wonderful freezer stand-by for pasta and many other dishes.

Makes 750 ml/1¼ pints/
3⅔ cups

INGREDIENTS
2 x 400 g/14 oz cans chopped tomatoes
60 ml/4 tbsp olive oil
2 garlic cloves, crushed
10 ml/2 tsp fresh thyme
10 ml/2 tsp anchovy essence (optional)
2.5 ml/½ tsp black olive paste (optional)
2.5 ml/½ tsp freshly ground black pepper

1 Empty the tomatoes into a nylon sieve set over a bowl. The juices will run clear after a short time. Allow the tomatoes to thicken for 10 minutes.

2 Heat the oil and garlic in a saucepan and add the thyme, sieved tomatoes, anchovy essence and olive paste, if using. Simmer for 5 minutes, then season lightly with pepper. Process in a blender if you like a smooth sauce. Cool, transfer to a rigid container and freeze.

Defrost in a cool place for 3–4 hours or overnight in the fridge. Return to a saucepan and reheat, stirring occasionally. Alternatively, defrost and reheat in the microwave.

Fruit Sauce

Make batches of this sauce when the fruits are in season, and serve with ice cream, mousse and other desserts.

Makes 300 ml/½ pint/1¼ cups

INGREDIENTS
450 g/1 lb fresh fruit, such as raspberries, strawberries, mangoes, peaches and kiwi fruit
15 ml/1 tbsp lemon juice
30–45 ml/2–3 tbsp caster sugar
30–45 ml/2–3 tbsp fruit brandy or liqueur (optional)

Put the fruit, lemon juice and sugar in a food processor fitted with the metal blade. Process for 1 minute, scraping down the sides once. Press the fruit purée through a fine sieve into a small bowl. Transfer the sauce to a rigid container and freeze.

Defrost in a cool place for 4 hours or overnight in the fridge. Stir in the brandy or liqueur and serve chilled. Do not defrost in the microwave.

Italian Pea & Basil Soup

This easy-to-make soup retains its fresh, summery taste well.

Serves 4

INGREDIENTS
75 ml/5 tbsp/⅓ cup olive oil
2 large onions, chopped
1 celery stick, chopped
1 carrot, chopped
1 garlic clove, finely chopped
400 g/14 oz/3½ cups petit pois
900 ml/1½ pints/3¾ cups vegetable stock
25 g/1 oz/1 cup fresh basil leaves, torn
salt and freshly ground black pepper
freshly grated Parmesan cheese and fresh
    basil leaves, to garnish

1 Heat the oil in a saucepan and add the onions, celery, carrot and garlic. Cover and cook over a low heat, stirring occasionally, for 45 minutes, or until the vegetables are soft. Add the peas and stock, and bring to the boil. Lower the heat, add the basil, season and simmer for 10 minutes.

2 Process the soup in a blender or food processor until smooth. Cool, pour into a rigid container and freeze.

Defrost for 5–6 hours or in the fridge overnight. Reheat over a low heat. Alternatively, defrost and reheat in the microwave. Garnish and serve.

Red Lentil & Coconut Soup

The flavour of virtually all pulses improves with freezing.

Serves 4

INGREDIENTS
30 ml/2 tbsp sunflower oil
2 red onions, finely chopped
1 bird's eye chilli, seeded and finely sliced
2 garlic cloves, chopped
200 g/7 oz/scant 1 cup red lentils, rinsed
5 ml/1 tsp ground coriander
5 ml/1 tsp paprika
400 ml/14 fl oz/1⅔ cups coconut milk
900 ml/1½ pints/3¾ cups water
juice of 1 lime
2 spring onions, chopped
75 ml/5 tbsp finely chopped fresh coriander
1 chopped spring onion and 45 ml/3 tbsp
    finely chopped fresh coriander, to garnish

1 Heat the oil and cook the onions, chilli and garlic, stirring, for 5 minutes. Stir in the lentils, spices, coconut milk and water. Bring to the boil, stir and simmer for 40–45 minutes.

2 Add the lime juice, spring onions and coriander. Cool, pour into a rigid container and freeze.

Defrost for 5–6 hours or overnight in the fridge. Reheat over a low heat. Alternatively, defrost and reheat in the microwave. Garnish and serve.

Fresh Tomato & Bean Soup

All kinds of beans freeze well, and this soup will retain its deliciously chunky texture for at least one month.

Serves 4

INGREDIENTS
900 g/2 lb ripe plum tomatoes
30 ml/2 tbsp olive oil
275 g/10 oz/1⅓ cups onions,
    roughly chopped
2 garlic cloves, crushed
900 ml/1½ pints/3¾ cups
    vegetable stock
30 ml/2 tbsp sun-dried tomato paste
10 ml/2 tsp paprika
15 ml/1 tbsp cornflour
30 ml/2 tbsp water
425 g/15 oz can cannellini beans,
    rinsed and drained
salt and freshly ground
    black pepper
30 ml/2 tbsp chopped fresh coriander,
    to garnish

1 First, peel the tomatoes. Using a sharp knife, make a small cross in each one and place in a bowl. Pour over boiling water to cover, and leave to stand for 30–60 seconds.

2 Drain the tomatoes and peel off the skins. Quarter them and then cut each piece in half again.

3 Heat the oil in a large saucepan. Add the onions and garlic, and cook for 3 minutes, or until just beginning to soften.

4 Add the tomatoes, stock, sun-dried tomato paste and paprika. Season lightly. Bring to the boil and simmer for 10 minutes.

5 Mix the cornflour to a paste with the water. Stir the beans into the soup with the cornflour paste. Cook for a further 5 minutes. Cool, pour into a rigid container and freeze.

Defrost for 6–7 hours or overnight in the fridge. Reheat over a low heat. Alternatively, defrost and reheat in the microwave. Serve hot, garnished with chopped coriander.

Hummus

Home-made hummus is a perfect dinner-party starter, and can be made up to two weeks in advance and frozen.

Serves 4–6

INGREDIENTS
150 g/5 oz/¾ cup dried chick-peas
juice of 2 lemons
2 garlic cloves, sliced
30 ml/2 tbsp olive oil
pinch of cayenne pepper
150 ml/¼ pint/⅔ cup
  tahini paste
salt and freshly ground
  black pepper

FOR SERVING
olive oil
cayenne pepper
flat leaf parsley

1 Put the chick-peas in a bowl with plenty of cold water and leave to soak for 8 hours or overnight.

2 Drain the chick-peas and cover with fresh water in a saucepan. Bring to the boil, reduce the heat and simmer gently for 2–2¼ hours, until soft. Drain.

3 Process the chick-peas in a food processor to a smooth purée. Add the lemon juice, garlic, olive oil, cayenne pepper, seasoning and tahini, and blend until creamy, scraping the mixture down from the sides of the bowl.

4 Transfer the hummus to a bowl, cover with foil or two layers of clear film and freeze.

Defrost for at least 6 hours or in the fridge overnight. Do not defrost in the microwave. Stir, sprinkle with olive oil and cayenne, and garnish.

Falafel

Perfect party food, these spicy fritters can be frozen for up to four weeks in advance, then deep-fried when required.

Serves 4

INGREDIENTS
150 g/5 oz/³⁄₄ cup dried chick-peas, soaked overnight in cold water and drained
1 large onion, coarsely chopped
2 garlic cloves, coarsely chopped
60 ml/4 tbsp coarsely chopped parsley
5 ml/1 tsp cumin seeds, crushed
5 ml/1 tsp coriander seeds, crushed
2.5 ml/½ tsp baking powder
salt and freshly ground black pepper
oil, for deep-frying
pitta bread, salad and yogurt, to serve

1 Put the drained chick-peas in a saucepan and cover with cold water. Bring to the boil, reduce the heat and simmer for about 2–2¼ hours, until soft. Drain thoroughly.

2 Place the chick-peas in a food processor with the onion, garlic, parsley, cumin, coriander, baking powder and seasoning. Process to a firm paste.

3 Shape the mixture into walnut-size balls and then flatten them slightly with your hand. Place in a rigid container or on a tray, cover with foil or two layers of clear film and freeze.

Defrost for 5–6 hours or overnight in the fridge. To serve, heat about 5 cm/2 in oil in a saucepan until sizzling. Fry the falafel in batches until golden. Drain on kitchen paper and keep hot while frying the remainder. Serve warm in pitta bread with salad and yogurt.

Crab Cakes

Unlike some seafood, crab freezes well and loses little of its texture, but you should still handle the cakes gently when thawed.

Makes about 15

INGREDIENTS
225 g/8 oz fresh white crab meat
115 g/4 oz/1⅓ cups cooked
    potatoes, mashed
30 ml/2 tbsp fresh herb seasoning
2.5 ml/½ tsp mild mustard
2.5 ml/½ tsp freshly ground
    black pepper
½ hot chilli pepper
15 ml/1 tbsp shrimp paste (optional)
2.5 ml/½ tsp dried oregano, crushed
1 egg, beaten
flour, for dusting
oil, for frying
lime wedges and basil leaves,
    to garnish

FOR THE TOMATO DIP
15 g/½ oz/1 tbsp butter or margarine
½ onion, finely chopped
2 canned plum tomatoes, chopped
1 garlic clove, crushed
150 ml/¼ pint/⅔ cup water
5–10 ml/1–2 tsp malt vinegar
15 ml/1 tbsp chopped
    fresh coriander
½ hot chilli pepper, chopped

1 To make the crab cakes, mix together the crab meat, potatoes, herb seasoning, mustard, peppers, shrimp paste, if using, oregano and egg in a large bowl. Chill for 30 minutes.

2 Make the tomato dip. Melt the butter or margarine in a small pan. Add the onion, tomatoes and garlic, and sauté for about 5 minutes, until the onion is soft. Add the water, vinegar, coriander and hot pepper. Simmer for 10 minutes.

3 Remove the dip from the heat and set aside to cool slightly. Transfer to a food processor or blender and process to a smooth purée. Transfer the dip to a bowl, set aside to cool completely, then cover with foil or two layers of clear film and freeze.

4 Using a spoon, shape the crab mixture into rounds and dust with flour. Place in a single layer in a rigid container or on a tray, cover with foil or two layers of clear film and freeze. The crab cakes may be transferred to a plastic freezer bag when frozen.

Defrost the crab cakes and the dip for 2–3 hours in the fridge. Alternatively, the crab cakes may be cooked from frozen. Do not defrost the crab cakes in the microwave, but the dip may be defrosted and reheated in the microwave, if serving hot. The dip may also be reheated in a saucepan over a low heat.

To serve, heat some oil in a frying pan and fry the crab cakes, for 3-4 minutes on each side, if defrosted, or 4–6 minutes on each side, if frozen. Drain on kitchen paper and keep warm while frying the remainder. Serve the crab cakes with warm or cold tomato dip and garnished with lime wedges and fresh basil leaves.

Spicy Beef Samosas

These deep-fried spicy fritters can be reheated straight from frozen within minutes in the microwave.

Serves 4

INGREDIENTS
15 ml/1 tbsp oil
115 g/4 oz/1 cup minced beef
3 spring onions, sliced
50 g/2 oz baby sweetcorn,
    finely chopped
1 carrot, diced
2.5 ml/½ tsp ground cumin
2.5 ml/½ tsp ground coriander
5 ml/1 tsp curry paste
50 ml/2 fl oz/¼ cup beef stock
6 sheets filo pastry, thawed
    if frozen
25 g/1 oz/2 tbsp melted butter
oil for deep-frying

FOR SERVING
fresh coriander
pickle

2 Add the spring onions, sweetcorn, carrot, cumin, coriander and curry paste. Cook for a further 5 minutes. Add the stock and bring to the boil.

3 Cover the sheets of filo with a damp dish towel and work on them one at a time to prevent them from drying out. Cut each filo sheet into eight. Brush one piece of pastry with melted butter and lay another sheet on top. Brush with butter and repeat to make eight stacks of pastry. Place one-eighth of the filling in the centre of each square of pastry and brush the pastry edges with butter. Fold into a triangle. Brush with melted butter.

1 Heat the oil in a heavy-based frying pan. Add the minced beef and fry, stirring occasionally, for 5 minutes, until brown and sealed.

4 Heat the oil for deep-frying in a large heavy-based pan to 180°C/350°F or until a cube of day-old bread browns in 30 seconds. Cook the samosas for 5 minutes, until golden brown. Drain well and cool. Place the samosas on a tray, cover with foil or two layers of clear film and freeze. When frozen, the samosas may be transferred to a plastic freezer bag.

Defrosting and reheating the samosas in the microwave is the easiest and most successful method. Alternatively, partially defrost in a cool place for 2–3 hours, then reheat in a preheated oven at 180°C/350°F/Gas 4 for 12–15 minutes, or until piping hot. Garnish with coriander, and serve with pickle.

Seafood Stew

It is important to allow this rich stew to defrost slowly and completely to ensure that the fish does not disintegrate.

Serves 6–8

INGREDIENTS

45 ml/3 tbsp olive oil
1 medium onion, sliced
1 carrot, sliced
½ celery stick, sliced
2 garlic cloves, chopped
1 x 400 g/14 oz can plum tomatoes,
    chopped, with their juice
225 g/8 oz fresh prawns, peeled and
    deveined (reserve the shells)
450 g/1 lb white fish bones and heads,
    gills removed
1 bay leaf
1 sprig fresh thyme, or ¼ tsp dried
    thyme leaves
a few peppercorns
750 g/1¾ lb fresh mussels, in their shells,
    scrubbed and rinsed
500 g/1¼ lb fresh small clams, in their shells,
    scrubbed and rinsed
250 ml/8 fl oz/1 cup white wine
1 kg/2 lb mixed fish fillets,
    such as cod, monkfish, red mullet
    or hake, bones removed and cut
    into chunks
salt and freshly ground black pepper

FOR SERVING

45 ml/3 tbsp finely chopped
    fresh parsley
rounds of French bread, toasted

1 Heat the oil in a medium saucepan. Add the onion and cook over a low heat until soft. Stir in the carrot and celery, and cook for 5 minutes more. Add the garlic, tomatoes and their juice, and 250 ml/8 fl oz/1 cup water. Cook over a moderate heat for about 15 minutes, until the vegetables are soft. Process in a food processor or pass through a food mill. Set the sauce aside.

2 Place the prawn shells in a large saucepan with the fish bones and heads. Add the herbs and peppercorns, and pour in 750 ml/1¼ pints/3⅔ cups water. Bring to the boil, reduce the heat and simmer for 25 minutes, skimming off any scum that rises to the surface. Strain and pour into a pan with the tomato sauce. Season lightly.

3 Place the mussels and clams in a saucepan with the wine. Cover, and steam until all the shells have opened. Discard any that do not open.

4 Lift the clams and mussels out and set aside. Filter the cooking liquid through a layer of paper towel and add it to the stock and tomato sauce.

5 Bring the sauce to the boil. Add the fish chunks and simmer for 2 minutes. Stir in the prawns, mussels and clams and remove from the heat. Cool, transfer to a rigid container and freeze.

Defrost in a cool place for 5–6 hours or overnight in the fridge. Reheat over a low heat, gently stirring occasionally. The stew can be defrosted and reheated in the microwave if you are in a hurry. Transfer to a warm serving dish, sprinkle with parsley and serve with toasted rounds of French bread.

Herby Plaice Croquettes

Why not make a large batch of these scrumptious croquettes and defrost them as and when they are needed?

Serves 4

INGREDIENTS
450 g/1 lb plaice fillets
300 ml/½ pint/1¼ cups milk
450 g/1 lb cooked potatoes
1 bulb fennel, finely chopped
1 garlic clove, finely chopped
45 ml/3 tbsp chopped fresh parsley
2 eggs
15 g/½ oz/1 tbsp unsalted butter
225 g/8 oz/4 cups white breadcrumbs
25 g/1 oz/2 tbsp sesame seeds
salt and freshly ground black pepper

FOR SERVING
oil, for deep-frying

1 Poach the fish fillets in the milk for about 15 minutes, until the fish flakes. Drain the fillets and reserve the milk.

VARIATION: If plaice is unavailable, other white fish, such as sole, haddock or cod, could be used.

2 Peel the skin off the fish and remove any bones. In a food processor fitted with a metal blade, process the fish, potatoes, fennel, garlic, parsley, eggs and butter.

3 Add 30 ml/2 tbsp of the reserved cooking milk, process briefly again and season lightly.

4 Chill in the fridge for 30 minutes, then shape into 20 croquettes using lightly floured hands.

Defrost for 2–3 hours in the fridge or cook from frozen. Heat the oil in a large heavy-based saucepan to 180°C/350°F or until a cube of day-old bread browns in 30 seconds. Fry the croquettes, in batches, for about 4 minutes, if defrosted, or for 6–8 minutes if still frozen. Drain on kitchen paper and serve hot.

5 Mix together the breadcrumbs and sesame seeds. Roll the croquettes in the mixture to form a good coating. Place in a rigid container or on a tray, cover with foil or two layers of clear film and freeze. The croquettes may be transferred to a plastic freezer bag when frozen.

Tuna Lasagne

Preparing and freezing this lasagne in advance takes all the time-consuming hard work away when supper time comes around.

Serves 6

INGREDIENTS
350 g/12 oz oven-ready
   dried lasagne
15 g/½ oz/1 tbsp butter
1 small onion, finely chopped
1 garlic clove, finely chopped
115 g/4 oz/1½ cups thinly
   sliced mushrooms
60 ml/4 tbsp dry white wine
150 ml/¼ pint/⅔ cup double cream
45ml/3 tbsp chopped fresh parsley
2 x 200 g/7 oz cans tuna, drained
2 canned pimientos, drained and
   cut into strips
75 g/3 oz/¾ cup frozen peas, thawed
115 g/4 oz/1 cup grated
   Mozzarella cheese
25 g/1 oz/⅓ cup grated
   Parmesan cheese
salt and freshly ground
   black pepper

FOR THE WHITE SAUCE
40 g/1½ oz/3 tbsp butter
40 g/1½ oz/⅓ cup plain flour
600 ml/1 pint/2½ cups milk
pinch of grated nutmeg

1 Soak the lasagne in a bowl of hot water for 3–5 minutes. Lift out into a colander and rinse with cold water. Lay the sheets on a dish towel, in one layer, to drain.

2 To make the white sauce, melt the butter in a heavy-based saucepan over a low heat. Stir in the flour to make a smooth paste and cook, stirring constantly, for 1 minute. Remove the pan from the heat and beat in about one-quarter of the milk, using a whisk. When the mixture is smooth, mix in the remaining milk.

3 Return the pan to a medium heat and bring to the boil, beating constantly. Lower the heat and simmer, beating frequently, for 5–10 minutes, until thickened and smooth. Stir in the nutmeg. Remove the pan from the heat and set aside.

4 Melt the butter in a saucepan. Cook the onion until soft. Add the garlic and mushrooms and cook until soft, stirring occasionally.

5 Pour in the wine, bring to the boil and boil for 1 minute. Add the white sauce, cream and parsley. Season lightly.

6 Spoon a thin layer of sauce over the base of a 30 x 23 cm/12 x 9 in ovenproof and freezerproof dish. Cover with a layer of lasagne. Flake the tuna. Scatter half of the tuna, pimiento strips, peas and Mozzarella over the pasta. Spoon one-third of the remaining sauce evenly over the top and cover with another layer of lasagne.

7 Repeat the layers, ending with pasta and sauce. Sprinkle with the Parmesan. Cool, cover with foil or two layers of clear film and freeze.

Defrost for 8–10 hours or for 12–15 hours in the fridge. Do not defrost in the microwave. To serve, bake in a preheated oven at 180°C/350°C/Gas 4 for about 30–40 minutes, until the top is golden brown and bubbling. Cut the lasagne into squares and serve straight from the dish.

25

Layered Fish Casserole

This is a wonderfully warming dish to come home to on a cold winter's evening, and all the better if all you have to do is heat it in the oven.

Serves 6–8

INGREDIENTS
750 ml/1¼ pints/3⅔ cups milk
1 slice onion
2–3 sprigs of fresh parsley
1 bay leaf
a few black peppercorns
65 g/2½ oz/5 tbsp butter
65 g/2½ oz/9 tbsp plain flour
2.5 ml/½ tsp grated lemon rind
1 egg, lightly beaten
150 g/5 oz/1⅔ cups coarsely crushed
    water biscuits
675 g/1½ lb skinless white fish fillets,
    finely diced
225 g/8 oz skinless smoked
    haddock or whiting fillet, cut
    into strips
salt and freshly ground
    black pepper

FOR SERVING
15 g/½ oz/1 tbsp butter, diced
sprigs of flat leaf parsley

1 Bring the milk to the boil with the onion, herbs and peppercorns. Remove from the heat and let stand for 20 minutes to infuse. Melt the butter in a separate pan, stir in the flour, then strain in the milk. Bring to the boil, whisking constantly, then simmer until thickened.

2 Remove the pan from the heat. Add the lemon rind and egg and mix well. Season lightly.

3 Scatter about one-third of the biscuit crumbs over the base of a buttered ovenproof and freezerproof dish. Cover with a layer of half the diced fish. Spoon half the sauce over the fish and arrange the strips of smoked fish on top. Repeat the layers of crumbs, white fish and sauce.

4 Scatter the remaining biscuit crumbs over the surface. Cool, cover with foil or two layers of clear film and freeze.

VARIATION: For fish pie, omit the biscuits and egg. Fold the diced fish into the sauce. Put half in a buttered ovenproof dish and cover with a layer of smoked fish strips. Top with the remaining fish mixture. Cover with mashed potato and freeze, covered with foil. Defrost, dot with butter and bake as shown right.

Defrost in a cool place for 8–10 hours or 12–15 hours in the fridge. Do not defrost in the microwave. To serve, dot the top with the diced butter and bake in a preheated oven at 180°C/350°F/ Gas 4 for about 35 minutes, until golden on top and bubbling around the edges. Garnish with the parsley.

Fish Parcels

This dish is an especially good choice for the freezer, as the flavours intermingle and infuse the flesh of the fish.

Serves 4

INGREDIENTS
4 pieces sea bass fillet or 4 whole small
    sea bass, about 450 g/1 lb each
oil, for brushing
2 shallots, thinly sliced
1 garlic clove, chopped
15 ml/1 tbsp capers
6 sun-dried tomatoes,
    finely chopped
4 black olives, stoned and
    thinly sliced
grated rind and juice of 1 lemon
5 ml/1 tsp paprika
salt and freshly ground black pepper
flat leaf parsley, to garnish

1 Clean the fish if whole. Cut four large squares of double-thickness foil, large enough to enclose the fish, and brush with a little oil.

2 Place a piece of fish in the centre of each piece of foil and season well with salt and pepper.

3 Scatter over the shallots, garlic, capers, tomatoes, olives and grated lemon rind. Sprinkle with the lemon juice and paprika.

4 Fold the foil over to enclose the fish loosely, sealing the edges firmly so none of the juices can escape. Place the parcels in the freezer and freeze.

Defrost in the fridge for up to 12 hours. Do not defrost in the microwave. To serve, place the parcels on a baking sheet and bake in a preheated oven at 200°C/400°F/ Gas 6 for 15–20 minutes. Open up the tops and serve. The parcels may also be cooked on a moderately hot barbecue for 8–10 minutes.

VARIATION: You could also use small whole trout or white fish fillets, such as cod or haddock, for this recipe.

Enchiladas with Hot Chilli Sauce

Freezing will make the chillies in this spicy Mexican dish more pungent, so use them with caution.

Serves 4

INGREDIENTS
8 wheat tortillas
175 g/6 oz/1½ cups grated Cheddar cheese
1 onion, finely chopped
350 g/12 oz cooked chicken, cut into
　small chunks
120 ml/4 fl oz/½ cup soured cream

FOR THE *SALSA PICANTE*
1–2 green chillies
15 ml/1 tbsp vegetable oil
1 onion, chopped
1 garlic clove, crushed
400 g/14 oz can chopped tomatoes
30 ml/2 tbsp tomato purée
salt and freshly ground black pepper

FOR SERVING
175 ml/6 fl oz/¾ cup soured cream
1 avocado, sliced and tossed in lemon juice

1 To make the *salsa picante,* cut the chillies in half lengthways and carefully remove the cores and seeds. Slice the chillies very finely. Heat the oil in a frying pan and fry the onion and garlic for about 3–4 minutes, until softened. Add the tomatoes, tomato purée and chillies. Simmer gently, uncovered, stirring frequently, for about 12–15 minutes.

2 Pour the sauce into a food processor or blender, and process until smooth. Return to the heat and cook very gently, uncovered, for a further 15 minutes. Season lightly, then set aside.

3 Butter a shallow ovenproof and freezerproof dish. Take one tortilla and sprinkle with a good pinch of cheese and chopped onion, about 40 g/1½ oz of chicken and 15 ml/1 tbsp of *salsa picante.* Pour over 15 ml/1 tbsp of soured cream, roll up and place, seam side down, in the dish. Repeat to make seven more enchiladas.

Defrost for 5–6 hours or overnight in the fridge. To serve, bake in a preheated oven at 180°C/350°F/ Gas 4 for 25–30 minutes, until golden. Alternatively, defrost and reheat in the microwave. Serve with soured cream and garnish with sliced avocado.

4 Pour the remaining *salsa* over the enchiladas, and sprinkle with the remaining cheese and onion. Cover with foil or two layers of clear film and freeze.

Chicken Pasties

Pastry is perfect for freezing and, because the chicken is boneless, the pasties can be cooked from frozen.

Serves 4

INGREDIENTS
350 g/12 oz/3 cups
    self-raising flour
2.5 ml/½ tsp salt
75 g/3 oz/6 tbsp lard
75 g/3 oz/6 tbsp butter
60–75 ml/4–5 tbsp cold water

FOR THE FILLING
450 g/1 lb boneless, skinless
    chicken thighs
25 g/1 oz/¼ cup chopped walnuts
25 g/1 oz/⅓ cup spring onions, sliced
50 g/2 oz/½ cup
    Stilton, crumbled
25 g/1 oz/¼ cup celery, finely chopped
2.5 ml/½ tsp dried thyme
salt and freshly ground
    black pepper

FOR SERVING
1 egg, lightly beaten

1 Mix the flour and salt in a bowl. Rub in the lard and butter with your fingers until the mixture resembles fine breadcrumbs. Using a knife to cut and stir, mix in the cold water to form a stiff, pliable dough.

2 Turn out on to a worktop and knead lightly until smooth. Divide into four equal pieces and roll out each piece to a thickness of 5 mm/¼ in, keeping a good round shape. Cut into a 20 cm/8 in circle, using a plate as a guide.

3 Remove any fat from the chicken thighs and cut into small cubes. Mix with the walnuts, spring onions, Stilton, celery, thyme and seasoning, and divide between the four pastry circles.

Defrost in a cool place for 2–3 hours or overnight in the fridge or cook from frozen. Do not defrost in the microwave. To serve, place the pasties on a baking sheet and brush with beaten egg to glaze. Bake in a preheated oven at 200°C/400°F/ Gas 6 for 45 minutes. If cooking from frozen, reduce the oven temperature to 180°C/350°F/Gas 4 and bake for a further 20–30 minutes. Serve the pasties hot or cold.

4 Brush the edge of the pastry with water and fold over, pinching and crimping the edges together well. Wrap the pasties in foil or two layers of clear film and freeze.

Chicken Curry

The spices in this curry will become stronger in the freezer, but do not store for more than three months or they will deteriorate.

Serves 4

INGREDIENTS
45 ml/3 tbsp vegetable oil
8 small onions, halved
2 bay leaves
8 green cardamom pods
4 cloves
3 dried red chillies
8 black peppercorns
2 onions, finely chopped
2 garlic cloves, crushed
2.5 cm/1 in piece of fresh root ginger,
    finely chopped
5 ml/1 tsp ground coriander
5 ml/1 tsp ground cumin
2.5 ml/½ tsp ground turmeric
5 ml/1 tsp chilli powder
2.5 ml/½ tsp salt
4 tomatoes, peeled and finely chopped
120 ml/4 fl oz/½ cup water
8 chicken pieces, such as thighs and
    drumsticks, skinned
plain rice, to serve

1 Heat 30 ml/2 tbsp of the oil in a large saucepan and fry the small onions for 10 minutes, or until golden brown. Remove and set aside.

COOK'S TIP: Soak the small onions in boiling water for 2–3 minutes to make them easier to peel.

2 Add the remaining oil and fry the bay leaves, cardamoms, cloves, chillies and peppercorns for 2 minutes. Add the chopped onions, garlic and ginger, and fry for 5 minutes. Stir in the ground spices and salt, and cook for 2 minutes.

3 Add the tomatoes and the water, and simmer for 5 minutes until the sauce thickens. Add the chicken and cook for about 5 minutes.

Defrost in a cool place for 5–6 hours or overnight in the fridge. Transfer to a saucepan and simmer, stirring occasionally, for 15 minutes, until the chicken is tender and cooked through. Alternatively, defrost and finish cooking in the microwave. Serve with plain boiled rice.

4 Add the reserved small onions, then cover and cook for a further 15 minutes. Cool, transfer to a rigid container and freeze.

Cassoulet

This traditional French dish is perfect for preparing when you have plenty of time and then freezing for another occasion.

Serves 6

INGREDIENTS
450 g/1 lb boneless duck breast
225 g/8 oz thick-cut streaky pork or
    unsmoked streaky bacon rashers
450 g/1 lb Toulouse or garlic sausages
45 ml/3 tbsp oil
450 g/1 lb/2 cups onions, chopped
2 garlic cloves, crushed
2 x 425 g/15 oz cans cannellini beans, rinsed
    and drained
225 g/8 oz/1¼ cups carrots, roughly chopped
400 g/14 oz can chopped tomatoes
15 ml/1 tbsp tomato purée
1 bouquet garni
30 ml/2 tbsp chopped fresh thyme
475 ml/16 fl oz/2 cups chicken stock
salt and pepper

FOR SERVING
115 g/4 oz/2 cups fresh breadcrumbs
fresh thyme sprigs,
    to garnish (optional)

1 Preheat the oven to 170°C/325°F/ Gas 3. Cut the duck breast and pork or bacon rashers into large pieces. Twist the sausages and cut into short lengths.

2 Heat the oil in a large flameproof casserole. Cook the meat in batches, until well browned. Remove from the pan using a slotted spoon, and drain on kitchen paper.

3 Add the onions and garlic to the pan and cook, stirring frequently, for 3–4 minutes, or until beginning to soften.

4 Stir in the beans, carrots, tomatoes, tomato purée, bouquet garni and thyme, and season to taste with salt and pepper. Return the meat to the pan and mix until well combined.

Defrost in a cool place for 5–6 hours or overnight in the fridge. Transfer the cassoulet to a casserole and sprinkle over the breadcrumbs. Cook, uncovered, in a preheated oven at 170°C/325°F/Gas 3 for 40 minutes, until the meat is tender and the topping is crisp. (If necessary, brown it under the grill.) Garnish with thyme, if using, and serve with salad leaves. Alternatively, defrost and finish cooking in the microwave, then brown the topping under the grill, garnish and serve.

5 Add enough of the stock to just cover the meat and beans. (The cassoulet shouldn't be swimming in juices; if the mixture becomes too dry, add a little more stock or water.) Bring to the boil. Cover tightly and cook in the oven for 1 hour. Cool, remove and discard the bouquet garni. Transfer the cassoulet to a rigid container and freeze.

Braised Lamb with Apricots & Herb Dumplings

Thanks to the freezer, this slow-cooked, tender casserole makes a perfect midweek supper for a cold night.

Serves 6

INGREDIENTS
30 ml/2 tbsp sunflower oil
675 g/1½ lb lean lamb fillet, cut into
  2.5 cm/1 in cubes
350 g/12 oz/4½ cups button onions, peeled
1 garlic clove, crushed
225 g/8 oz/3 cups button mushrooms
175 g/6 oz/¾ cup small ready-to-eat
  dried apricots
about 250 ml/8 fl oz/1 cup lamb or
  beef stock
250 ml/8 fl oz/1 cup red wine
15 ml/1 tbsp tomato purée
salt and freshly ground black pepper
fresh herb sprigs, to garnish

FOR THE DUMPLINGS
115 g/4 oz/1 cup self-raising flour
50 g/2 oz/scant ½ cup shredded
  vegetable suet
15–30 ml/1–2 tbsp chopped fresh
  mixed herbs

1 Preheat the oven to 170°C/325°F/ Gas 3. Heat the oil in a large, flameproof casserole, add the lamb and cook gently until browned all over, stirring occasionally. Remove the meat from the casserole using a slotted spoon, set aside and keep warm.

2 Add the button onions, garlic and mushrooms to the oil remaining in the casserole and cook gently for about 5 minutes, stirring occasionally.

3 Return the meat to the casserole, add the dried apricots, lamb or beef stock, red wine and tomato purée. Season lightly and stir to mix.

Defrost the braised lamb and the dumplings for 8 hours or up to 15 hours in the fridge. Or, defrost the braised lamb, but not the dumplings, in the microwave. Transfer the lamb to a casserole. Arrange the dumplings on top and cook in a preheated oven at 190°C/375°F/ Gas 5 for 30–35 minutes, until the dumplings are cooked through and the casserole is piping hot. Alternatively, cook in the microwave. Garnish and serve immediately.

4 Bring to the boil, stirring, then remove the casserole from the heat and cover. Transfer the casserole to the oven and cook for 1½–2 hours, until the lamb is cooked and tender, stirring once or twice and adding a little extra stock, if necessary. Set aside to cool, then transfer to a rigid container and freeze.

5 To make the dumplings, place the flour, suet, herbs and seasoning in a bowl, and stir to mix. Add enough cold water to make a soft, elastic dough. Divide the dough into small, marble-size pieces and, using lightly floured hands, roll each piece into a small ball. Place the dumplings on a tray, cover with foil or two layers of clear film and freeze. They may be transferred to a plastic freezer bag when frozen.

Herbed Burgers

Home-made burgers are probably *the* great freezer stand-by.

Serves 4

INGREDIENTS
675 g/1½ lb/6 cups lean minced beef
1 garlic clove, finely chopped
1 spring onion, very finely chopped
45 ml/3 tbsp finely chopped fresh basil
30 ml/2 tbsp finely chopped fresh parsley
salt and freshly ground black pepper

FOR SERVING
40 g/1½ oz/3 tbsp butter
300 ml/½ pint/1¼ cups Tomato Sauce
flat leaf parsley, to garnish

1 Thoroughly combine the meat with the garlic, spring onion, basil and parsley in a large mixing bowl. Season lightly with salt and pepper.

2 Form into four burgers between the palms of your hands, transfer to a rigid container or a tray, cover with foil or two layers of clear film and freeze. When frozen, the burgers may be transferred to a plastic freezer bag.

Defrost in a cool place for 5–6 hours or overnight in the fridge. Do not defrost in the microwave. To serve, melt the butter in a frying pan. Add the burgers and cook over a moderate heat until browned on both sides, turning once. Garnish the burgers with a sprig of parsley, and serve with tomato sauce.

Beef Stew with Red Wine

Hearty stews develop a richness when stored in the freezer.

Serves 6

INGREDIENTS
75 ml/5 tbsp/⅓ cup olive oil
1.2 kg/2½ lb lean beef, diced
1 medium onion, very finely sliced
2 carrots, chopped
45 ml/3 tbsp finely chopped fresh parsley
1 garlic clove, chopped
1 bay leaf
a few sprigs fresh thyme
250 ml/8 fl oz/1 cup red wine
400 g/14 oz can chopped plum tomatoes
120 ml/4 fl oz/½ cup beef or chicken stock
about 15 black olives, stoned and halved
salt and freshly ground black pepper
1 large red pepper, cut into strips

1 Preheat the oven to 180°C/350°F/
Gas 4. Heat 45 ml/3 tbsp of the oil in
a casserole. Brown the meat, in batches.

2 Remove the meat and add the
remaining oil, onion and carrots. Cook
gently for 5 minutes. Add the parsley
and garlic, and cook for 3–4 minutes.

3 Return the meat and stir in the bay
leaf, thyme and wine. Bring to the
boil, stirring for 4–5 minutes. Stir in
the tomatoes, stock and olives, and
season. Cover and bake in the oven for
1½ hours. Allow to cool. Transfer to a
rigid container and freeze.

Defrost for 8 hours or in the fridge
for up to 15 hours. Transfer to a
casserole and stir in the pepper strips.
Cook, uncovered, in a preheated
oven at 180°C/350°C/Gas 4 for
30–40 minutes. Alternatively, defrost
and finish cooking in the microwave.

Pastitsio

Freeze this substantial Greek version of lasagne in a gratin dish, so all you have to do is defrost and heat it in the oven.

Serves 4–6

INGREDIENTS
225 g/8 oz/2¼ cups macaroni
30 ml/2 tbsp olive oil
1 large onion, finely chopped
2 garlic cloves, crushed
450 g/1 lb/4 cups minced steak
300 ml/½ pint/1¼ cups beef stock
10 ml/2 tsp tomato purée
5 ml/1 tsp ground cinnamon
5 ml/1 tsp ground cumin
15 ml/1 tbsp chopped fresh mint
50 g/2 oz/¼ cup butter
40 g/1½ oz/⅓ cup plain flour
120 ml/4 fl oz/½ cup milk
120 ml/4 fl oz/½ cup natural yogurt
175 g/6 oz/1½ cups grated Kefalotiri cheese
salt and freshly ground black pepper

1 Bring a saucepan of lightly salted water to the boil. Add the macaroni and cook for 8 minutes, or according to the instructions on the packet, until *al dente*. Drain, rinse under cold water and drain again. Set aside.

Defrost in a cool place for 8 hours or up to 15 hours in the fridge. Bake in a preheated oven at 190°C/375°F/Gas 5 for 45 minutes, until golden brown on top. Alternatively, defrost and finish cooking in the microwave, then brown under the grill.

2 Heat the oil in a frying pan, add the onion and garlic, and cook for 8–10 minutes, until soft. Add the minced steak and stir until browned. Stir in the stock, tomato purée, cinnamon, cumin and mint, and season lightly. Cook gently for 10–15 minutes, until the sauce is thick and flavoursome.

3 Melt the butter in a saucepan. Stir in the flour and cook for 1 minute. Remove the pan from the heat and gradually stir in the milk and yogurt. Return the pan to the heat and cook gently for 5 minutes. Stir in half the cheese and season lightly. Stir the macaroni into the cheese sauce.

VARIATION: If Kefalotiri cheese is unavailable, use a well-flavoured Cheddar cheese or similar.

4 Spread half the macaroni mixture over the base of a large freezerproof gratin dish. Cover with the meat sauce, and top with the remaining macaroni. Sprinkle the remaining cheese over the top. Cool, cover with foil or two layers of clear film and freeze.

43

Layered Polenta Bake

This is a good dish to prepare when you have some spare time, to freeze for an occasion when you will be very busy.

Serves 6

INGREDIENTS
5 ml/1 tsp salt
375 g/13 oz/3 cups fine polenta
olive oil, for greasing and brushing
25 g/1 oz/⅓ cup grated Parmesan cheese
salt and freshly ground black pepper

FOR THE TOMATO SAUCE
15 ml/1 tbsp olive oil
2 garlic cloves, chopped
400 g/14 oz/3 cups chopped tomatoes
15 ml/1 tbsp chopped fresh sage
2.5 ml/½ tsp soft brown sugar
200 g/7 oz/1½ cups canned cannellini beans,
    rinsed and drained

FOR THE SPINACH SAUCE
250 g/9 oz spinach, tough stalks removed
150 ml/¼ pint/⅔ cup single cream
115 g/4 oz/1 cup Gorgonzola cheese, cubed
large pinch of ground nutmeg

1 Bring 2 litres/3½ pints/8 cups water to the boil in a large saucepan and add the salt. Remove from the heat and slowly whisk in the polenta.

Defrost for 8 hours or in the fridge for up to 15 hours. Bake in a preheated oven at 190°C/375°F/ Gas 5 for 40 minutes, then place under a preheated grill until golden.

2 Return the pan to the heat and stir constantly for 15–20 minutes, until the polenta is thick and comes away from the side of the pan. Remove the pan from the heat.

3 Season lightly with pepper, then spoon the polenta on to a wet work surface or piece of marble. Using a wet spatula, spread out the polenta until it is 1 cm/½ in thick. Leave to cool for about 1 hour.

4 To make the tomato sauce, heat the oil in a saucepan, then fry the garlic for 1 minute. Add the tomatoes and sage and bring to the boil. Reduce the heat, add the sugar and seasoning, and simmer for 10 minutes, until slightly reduced, stirring occasionally. Stir in the beans and cook for a further 2 minutes.

5 Meanwhile, wash the spinach thoroughly and place in a large pan with only the water that clings to the leaves.

6 Cover and cook over a medium heat for about 3 minutes. Tip the spinach into a colander and drain, squeezing out the excess water.

7 Heat the cream, cheese and nutmeg in a small saucepan. Bring to the boil, reduce the heat and stir in the spinach and seasoning. Cook gently until slightly thickened, stirring frequently.

8 Cut the polenta into triangles. Place a layer of polenta in an oiled, deep ovenproof and freezerproof dish. Spoon over the tomato sauce, then top with another layer of polenta. Top with the spinach sauce and cover with the remaining polenta triangles. Brush with olive oil and sprinkle with Parmesan. Cool, cover with foil or two layers of clear film and freeze.

Sweet & Sour Mixed Bean Hot-pot

Freezing improves the flavour of this appetizing bean casserole, but do not store it for longer than about a month.

Serves 6

INGREDIENTS

450 g/1 lb unpeeled potatoes
15 ml/1 tbsp olive oil
40 g/1½ oz/3 tbsp butter
40 g/1½ oz/⅓ cup plain
    wholemeal flour
300 ml/½ pint/1¼ cups passata
150 ml/¼ pint/⅔ cup unsweetened
    apple juice
60 ml/4 tbsp each light soft brown sugar,
    tomato ketchup, dry sherry, cider vinegar
    and light soy sauce
400 g/14 oz can butter beans
400 g/14 oz can red kidney beans
400 g/14 oz can flageolet beans
400 g/14 oz can chick-peas
175 g/6 oz/1 cup green beans, chopped
    and blanched
225 g/8 oz/1 cup shallots, sliced
    and blanched
225 g/8 oz/3 cups mushrooms, sliced
15 ml/1 tbsp each chopped fresh thyme
    and marjoram
salt and freshly ground black pepper
fresh herb sprigs, to garnish

1 Thinly slice the potatoes and parboil them for 4 minutes. Drain thoroughly, toss them in the olive oil so they are lightly coated all over, and set aside.

2 Place the butter, flour, passata, apple juice, sugar, tomato ketchup, sherry, vinegar and soy sauce in a saucepan. Heat gently, whisking until the sauce comes to the boil and thickens. Simmer gently for 3 minutes, stirring.

3 Rinse and drain the beans and chick-peas and add to the sauce with all the remaining ingredients, except the herb garnish. Mix well.

Defrost for 8 hours or in the fridge for up to 15 hours. Cover with foil and bake in a preheated oven at 200°C/400°F/Gas 6 for 40 minutes. Remove the foil and bake for a further 20–30 minutes, until the potatoes are lightly browned. Garnish and serve. Alternatively, defrost and finish cooking in the microwave (do not cover with foil) and brown the topping under the grill.

4 Spoon the bean mixture into an ovenproof and freezerproof dish. Arrange the potato slices over the top, completely covering the bean mixture. Cool, cover with foil or two layers of clear film and freeze.

Spinach Pie

This pie is a great freezer stand-by, but take care not to crush the delicate pastry by putting anything on top.

Serves 6

INGREDIENTS
900 g/2 lb fresh spinach, chopped
25 g/1 oz/2 tbsp butter or margarine
2 onions, chopped
2 garlic cloves, crushed
275 g/10 oz/1¼ cups feta, grated
115 g/4 oz/¾ cup pine nuts
5 eggs, beaten
2 saffron strands, soaked in 30 ml/2 tbsp boiling water
5 ml/1 tsp paprika
1.5 ml/¼ tsp ground cumin
1.5 ml/¼ tsp ground cinnamon
14 sheets filo pastry, thawed if frozen
about 60 ml/4 tbsp olive oil
salt and freshly ground black pepper
lettuce, to serve

1 Place the spinach in a large colander, sprinkle with a little salt, rub into the leaves and leave for 30 minutes to drain the excess liquid.

Partially defrost in the fridge for 5–6 hours. Brush the top of the pie with a little water and bake in a preheated oven at 180°C/350°F/Gas 4 for 40–50 minutes, until the filling is cooked through and the pastry is golden brown. Serve with lettuce. Do not defrost or cook in the microwave.

2 Melt the butter or margarine in a large pan and fry the onions until golden. Add the garlic, cheese and nuts. Remove from the heat and stir in the eggs, spinach, saffron and spices. Season lightly and mix well.

3 Grease a large rectangular ovenproof and freezerproof dish. Take seven sheets of filo and brush one side with a little olive oil. Place on the base of the dish, overlapping the sides.

4 Spoon the spinach mixture over the pastry and carefully drizzle 30 ml/2 tbsp of the remaining olive oil over the top.

5 Fold the overlapping pastry over the filling. Cut the remaining pastry sheets to the dish size and brush each one with more olive oil. Arrange on top of the filling. Cool, cover with foil or two layers of clear film and freeze.

Tomato Casserole

Make the most of the wonderful flavour of sun-ripened tomatoes by freezing this casserole for when they are no longer in season.

Serves 4

INGREDIENTS
40 ml/2½ tbsp olive oil
45ml/3 tbsp chopped fresh flat
  leaf parsley
1 kg/2¼ lb firm ripe tomatoes
5 ml/1 tsp caster sugar
40 g/1½ oz/scant 1 cup day-old
  breadcrumbs
2.5 ml/½ tsp chilli powder
  or paprika
salt
chopped parsley, to garnish
rye bread, to serve

1 Brush a large ovenproof and freezerproof dish with 15 ml/1 tbsp of the oil.

2 Sprinkle the parsley over the base of the dish. Cut the tomatoes into even slices, discarding the end slices. Arrange the slices in the dish so that they overlap slightly. Sprinkle them with a little salt and the caster sugar.

3 In a mixing bowl, stir together the breadcrumbs, the remaining oil and chilli powder or paprika, then sprinkle over the top of the tomatoes. Cover with foil or two layers of clear film and freeze.

Defrost in a cool place for 5–6 hours or overnight in the fridge. Cook, uncovered, in a preheated oven at 200°C/400°F/Gas 6 for 40–50 minutes, covering the topping with foil if it is getting too browned. Garnish with parsley and serve with rye bread. Do not defrost or cook in the microwave.

COOK'S TIP: To vary this recipe, replace half the quantity of tomatoes with 450 g/1 lb courgettes. Slice the courgettes evenly and arrange alternate slices of courgette and tomato in the dish, overlapping the slices as before.

Apple & Blackcurrant Pancakes

Pancakes freeze perfectly stacked interleaved with greaseproof paper in a plastic freezer bag.

Makes 8

INGREDIENTS
115 g/4 oz/1 cup plain or wholemeal flour
300 ml/½ pint/1¼ cups milk
1 egg, beaten
15 ml/1 tbsp sunflower oil, plus extra
    for greasing

FOR THE FILLING
450 g/1 lb cooking apples
225 g/8 oz/2 cups blackcurrants
30–45 ml/2–3 tbsp water
30 ml/2 tbsp demerara sugar

FOR SERVING
melted butter
crème fraîche
chopped, toasted nuts or sesame seeds

1 Make the pancake batter. Place the flour in a mixing bowl and make a well in the centre.

2 Add a little of the milk with the egg and the oil. Whisk the flour into the liquid, then gradually whisk in the rest of the milk, until smooth. Cover the batter and chill while you prepare the filling.

3 Quarter, peel and core the apples. Slice them into a pan and add the blackcurrants and water. Cook over a low heat for 10–15 minutes, until the fruit is soft. Stir in enough demerara sugar to sweeten.

4 Lightly grease a pancake pan with oil. Heat the pan, pour in about 30 ml/2 tbsp batter, swirl it around and cook for about 1 minute. Flip the pancake over using a palette knife and cook the other side. Set aside on a plate. Cook the remaining pancakes.

5 Cool the pancakes, then place a square of greaseproof paper between each one. Put the pancakes flat in a plastic freezer bag and freeze. The filling should be frozen separately in a rigid container.

Defrost the pancakes in a cool place for 30 minutes and the sauce for 5-6 hours or overnight in the fridge. Transfer the pancakes to an ovenproof dish, fold them in half, brush with melted butter and cover with foil. Reheat in a preheated oven at 180°C/350°F/Gas 4 for about 15 minutes.

Alternatively, defrost and reheat in the microwave (do not cover with foil). Reheat the sauce in a saucepan or in the microwave.

To serve place two pancakes on a warmed plate and pour some of the sauce over them. Top with crème fraîche and chopped, toasted nuts or sesame seeds.

Plum Crumble Pie

Make this pie when plums are in season and freeze it for a delicious taste of autumn later in the year.

Serves 6–8

INGREDIENTS
115 g/4 oz/1 cup plain flour, sifted
115 g/4 oz/1 cup wholemeal flour
150 g/5 oz/¾ cup golden caster sugar
115 g/4 oz/1 cup polenta
5 ml/1 tsp baking powder
pinch of salt
150 g/5 oz/10 tbsp unsalted butter, plus extra
   for greasing
1 egg
15 ml/1 tbsp olive oil
25 g/1 oz/¼ cup rolled oats
15 ml/1 tbsp demerara sugar

FOR THE FILLING
10 ml/2 tsp caster sugar
15 ml/1 tbsp polenta
450 g/1 lb dark plums

1 Mix together the flours, sugar, polenta, baking powder and salt in a large bowl. Rub in the butter using your fingers until the mixture resembles fine breadcrumbs. Stir in the egg and olive oil, and enough cold water to form a smooth dough.

2 Grease a 23 cm/9 in spring-form cake tin. Press two-thirds of the dough evenly over the base and up the sides of the tin. Wrap the remaining dough in clear film and chill while you make the filling.

3 Preheat the oven to 180°C/350°F/ Gas 4. Sprinkle the caster sugar and polenta in the pastry case.

4 Cut the plums in half and remove the stones, then place the plums, cut-side down, on top of the polenta.

5 Remove the remaining dough from the fridge and crumble it between your fingers, then combine with the oats. Sprinkle the mixture evenly over the plums, then sprinkle the demerara sugar on top.

6 Bake for 50 minutes, or until golden. Leave for 15 minutes before removing the cake from the tin. Leave to cool on a wire rack. Wrap in foil or a plastic freezer bag and freeze.

Defrost in a cool place for 8 hours or up to 15 hours in the fridge. Serve at room temperature.

Apple Pie

A family favourite – why not make a double batch of this traditional apple pie, which loses none of its crispness and flavour in the freezer?

Serves 8

INGREDIENTS
900 g/2 lb tart cooking apples, such as Bramley, Jonathan, Granny Smith or Winesap
30 ml/2 tbsp plain flour
90 g/3½ oz/½ cup sugar
22.5 ml/4½ tsp lemon juice
2.5 ml/½ tsp ground cinnamon
2.5 ml/½ tsp ground allspice
1.5 ml/¼ tsp ground ginger
1.5 ml/¼ tsp grated nutmeg
1.5 ml/¼ tsp salt
50 g/2 oz/4 tbsp butter, diced

FOR THE CRUST
225 g/8 oz/2 cups plain flour
5 ml/1 tsp salt
75 g/3 oz/6 tbsp cold butter, diced
50 g/2 oz/4 tbsp cold vegetable shortening, diced
60–120 ml/4–8 tbsp iced water

1 For the crust, sift the flour and salt into a mixing bowl. Add the butter and shortening and cut in using a pastry blender or rub between your fingertips until the mixture resembles coarse crumbs.

2 Using a fork, stir in just enough water to bind the dough. Gather into two balls, wrap in greaseproof paper and chill for 20 minutes.

3 On a lightly floured surface, roll out one dough ball 3 mm/⅛ in thick. Transfer to a 23 cm/9 in pie tin and trim the edge. Place a baking sheet in the centre of the oven and preheat to 220°C/425°F/Gas 7.

4 Peel, core and slice the apples into a bowl. Toss with the flour, sugar, lemon juice, spices and salt. Spoon into the pie case and dot with butter.

5 Roll out the remaining dough. Place on top of the pie and trim to leave a 2 cm/¾ in overhang. Fold the overhang under the bottom dough and press to seal. Crimp the edge.

6 Roll out the trimmings and cut out leaf shapes and roll balls. Arrange on top of the pie. Cut steam vents.

7 Bake for 10 minutes. Reduce the heat to 180°C/350°F/Gas 4 and bake for 40–45 minutes more, until golden. If the pie browns too quickly, protect with foil. Cool, cover with foil or two layers of clear film and freeze.

Defrost in a cool place for 5–6 hours or overnight in the fridge. If serving hot, reheat in a preheated oven at 170°C/325°F/Gas 3 for 20 minutes. Cover the top with foil if the pastry is getting too brown. Alternatively, serve the pie at room temperature. Do not defrost or reheat the pie in the microwave.

Chocolate Cheesecake Pie

Take the effort out of entertaining by preparing this melt-in-the-mouth
dessert well in advance and then freezing it.

Serves 8

INGREDIENTS
350 g/12 oz/1½ cups cream cheese
60 ml/4 tbsp double cream
200 g/7 oz/1 cup sugar
50 g/2 oz/½ cup cocoa powder
2.5 ml/½ tsp ground cinnamon
3 eggs

FOR THE CRUST
50 g/2 oz/1 cup crushed
   digestive biscuits
25 g/1 oz/½ cup crushed
   amaretti biscuits
75 g/3 oz/6 tbsp butter, melted

FOR SERVING
whipped cream
chocolate curls

1 Place a large baking sheet in the
oven and preheat to 180°C/350°F/
Gas 4. For the crust, mix the biscuit
crumbs and butter in a bowl.

Defrost in a cool place for 5–6 hours
or overnight in the fridge. Decorate
with whipped cream and chocolate
curls and serve cold. Do not defrost
in the microwave.

2 Using a spoon, press the crumbs
evenly over the base and sides of a
23 cm/9 in flan tin. Bake for 8 minutes.
Let cool. Keep the oven on.

3 Using an electric mixer, beat the
cheese and cream together until
smooth. Beat in the sugar, cocoa and
cinnamon until blended. Add the
eggs, one at a time, beating just enough
to blend.

4 Pour into the flan tin and bake on the hot sheet for 25–30 minutes. Remove from the oven and cool. The filling will sink slightly. Cover with foil or two layers of clear film and freeze.

COOK'S TIP: If you like, use a mixture of dark and white chocolate for the decorative curls.

Sticky Coffee & Ginger Pudding

This light-as-air sponge pudding can be cooked from frozen and is delicious served with vanilla ice cream.

Serves 4

INGREDIENTS
30 ml/2 tbsp soft light brown sugar
25 g/1 oz/2 tbsp stem ginger, chopped
30 ml/2 tbsp mild-flavoured
    ground coffee
75 ml/5 tbsp/⅓ cup stem ginger syrup
    (from a jar of stem ginger)
115 g/4 oz/generous ½ cup
    caster sugar
3 eggs, separated
25 g/1 oz/¼ cup plain flour
5 ml/1 tsp ground ginger
65 g/2½ oz/generous 1 cup fresh
    white breadcrumbs
25 g/1 oz/¼ cup ground almonds
oil for greasing

2 Put the ground coffee in a small bowl. Heat the ginger syrup until almost boiling; pour it into the coffee, stir well and set aside for 4 minutes. Pour through a fine sieve into the pudding basin.

3 Beat half the caster sugar and egg yolks until light and fluffy. Sift the flour and ground ginger together and fold into the egg mixture with the breadcrumbs and ground almonds.

Remove the foil or clear film and cook the pudding from frozen in a preheated oven at 180°C/350°F/ Gas 4 for about 1 hour, or until firm to the touch and piping hot. Alternatively, cook the pudding from frozen in the microwave.

1 Grease the base of a 750 ml/ 1¼ pint/3⅔ cup ovenproof and freezerproof pudding basin, then sprinkle in the soft light brown sugar and chopped stem ginger.

4 Whisk the egg whites until stiff, then gradually whisk in the remaining caster sugar. Fold into the mixture, half at a time. Spoon into the pudding basin and smooth the top.

5 Cover the pudding basin with a piece of pleated, greased greaseproof paper and secure with string. Cover with foil or two layers of clear film and freeze.

Apricot & Walnut Loaf

An occasional baking session for the freezer is fun and will ensure a ready supply of tasty home-cooked treats.

Makes 10–12 slices

INGREDIENTS
225 g/8 oz/2 cups plain wholemeal flour
5 ml/1 tsp baking powder
pinch of salt
115 g/4 oz/½ cup sunflower margarine
175 g/6 oz/1 cup soft light brown sugar
2 eggs, lightly beaten
grated rind and juice of 1 orange
50 g/2 oz/½ cup chopped walnuts
50 g/2 oz/¼ cup ready-to-eat dried
   apricots, chopped
1 large cooking apple
oil, for greasing

1 Preheat the oven to 180°C/350°F/ Gas 4. Line and grease a 900 g/2 lb loaf tin.

2 Sift the flour, baking powder and salt into a bowl, then tip in the bran in the sieve. Add the margarine, sugar, eggs, orange rind and juice. Beat with an electric mixer until smooth.

3 Stir in the walnuts and apricots. Peel, core and chop the apple, and stir it in. Spoon the mixture into the prepared tin and level the top.

4 Bake for 1 hour, or until a skewer inserted in the centre comes out clean. Cool for 5 minutes, then turn out on to a wire rack and peel off the paper. When cold, wrap in foil and freeze.

Defrost in a cool place for 5–6 hours. Do not defrost in the microwave.

Pear & Sultana Teabread

The rich, fruity flavour of this moist teabread is accentuated by freezing, but do not store for more than one month.

Serves 6–8

INGREDIENTS
25 g/1 oz/scant ⅓ cup rolled oats
50 g/2 oz/⅓ cup light muscovado sugar
30 ml/2 tbsp pear or apple juice
30 ml/2 tbsp sunflower oil
1 large or 2 small pears
115 g/4 oz/1 cup self-raising flour
115 g/4 oz/⅔ cup sultanas
2.5 ml/½ tsp baking powder
10 ml/2 tsp mixed spice
1 egg

1 Preheat the oven to 180°C/350°F/ Gas 4. Grease and line a 450 g/1 lb loaf tin. Put the oats, sugar, juice and oil in a bowl, mix well and then set aside for 15 minutes.

2 Quarter, core and grate the pear(s). Add to the oat mixture with the flour, sultanas, baking powder, mixed spice and egg. Mix well.

3 Spoon the mixture into the prepared loaf tin and level the top using the back of a spoon.

4 Bake for 50–60 minutes, or until a skewer inserted into the centre comes out clean. Turn out on to a wire rack to cool, then wrap in foil and freeze.

Defrost in a cool place for 5–6 hours. Do not defrost in the microwave.

This edition published by Southwater

Distributed in the UK by
The Manning Partnership, 251–253 London Road East, Batheaston, Bath BA1 7RL, UK
tel. (0044) 01225 852 727   fax. (0044) 01225 852 852

Distributed in Australia by
Sandstone Publishing, Unit 1, 360 Norton Street, Leichhardt, New South Wales 2040, Australia
tel. (0061) 2 9560 7888 fax. (0061) 2 9560 7488

Distributed in New Zealand by
Five Mile Press NZ, PO Box 33-1071, Takapuna
Auckland 9, New Zealand
tel. (0064) 9 4444 144   fax. (0064) 9 4444 618

A CIP catalogue record for this book
is available from the British Library.

1 3 5 7 9 10 8 6 4 2

Publisher: Joanna Lorenz
Editor: Valerie Ferguson
Series Designer: Bobbie Colgate Stone
Designer: Andrew Heath
Editorial Reader: Richard McGinlay
Production Controller: Joanna King

Recipes contributed by: Catherine Atkinson,
Carla Capalbo, Lesley Chamberlain, Carole Clements,
Trisha Davies, Sarah Edmonds, Joanna Farrow,
Christine France, Nicola Graines, Rosamund Grant,
Carole Handslip, Christine Ingram, Manisha Kanani,
Soheila Kimberley, Patricia Lousada, Lesley Mackley,
Norma Macmillan, Sue Maggs, Maggie Pannell,
Anne Sheasby, Jenny Stacey, Liz Trigg,
Steven Wheeler, Elizabeth Wolf-Cohen

Photography: Karl Adamson, Louise Dove,
James Duncan, Ian Garlick, Michelle Garrett,
Amanda Heywood, David Jordan, Don Last,
William Lingwood, Patrick McLeavey, Thomas Odulate

Notes:
For all recipes, quantities are given in both metric
and imperial measures and, where appropriate,
measures are also given in standard cups
and spoons.
Follow one set, but not a mixture, because they
are not interchangeable.

Standard spoon and cup measures are level.

1 tsp = 5 ml   1 tbsp = 15 ml

1 cup = 250 ml/8 fl oz

Australian standard tablespoons are 20 ml.
Australian readers should use 3 tsp in place of
1 tbsp for measuring small quantities of gelatine,
cornflour, salt, etc.

Medium eggs are used unless otherwise stated.

Printed and bound in Singapore